WHO SAID THAT

WRITINGS FROM AN EMPTY ROOM

DR. RICHARD "RICK" RHODES

authorHOUSE

AuthorHouse™
1663 Liberty Drive
Bloomington, IN 47403
www.authorhouse.com
Phone: 833-262-8899

Published by AuthorHouse 06/02/2023

ISBN: 979-8-8230-0450-3 (sc)
ISBN: 979-8-8230-0449-7 (e)

*I UNDERSTAND THE REASONS
FOR WHICH THERE IS SOME
JUSTICE*

*BUT EVEN MORESO,
I DON'T UNDERSTAND REASONS
FOR WHICH THERE IS SO LITTLE*
Published 1984
(Dr. Richard Stewart Rhodes)

(see addendum)

NOTABLE QUOTATIONS

What a good thing Adam had. When he said
a good thing he knew nobody had said it before.
(Mark Twain)

Dorothy Parker once suggested, "We all assume
that Oscar said it."

I always have a question for everything,
it saves original thinking.
(Dorothy Sayers)

"It's a good thing for an uneducated man
to read books of quotations."
(Winston Churchill)

Proper words in proper places'
(Jonathan Swift)

"The arc of history is long but
it bends towards justice.
(Barack Obama)

"Wit is the salt of conversation, not the food."
(William Hazlitt)

"Wherever you go, go with all your heart."
(Confucius)

"Life is either a daring adventure or nothing."
(Helen Keller)

Some of these writings deserve an explanatory understanding. Please refer to addendum when noted.

Special thanks to Mr. & Mrs. Walter and Maesoa Darton
for their continuing contributions to those in need.

Special, thanks to all of those "First Responders," medical,
fire, police, clergy, genuine good Samaritans.

Thanks to all who care in times of disastrous need.

CONTENTS

This Book
Is
ESPECIALLY DEDICATED
To
My wife Gwen who was extremely
instrumental to this writing.
Her love, inspiration, support
and technical assistance;
guided me on to the completion of this manuscript.
Thanks "G"

SPECIAL ACKNOWLEDGEMENTS

Michael "Hap" O'Daniel   (Mentor, Journalist, Screenwriter)

Simone "Anika" Wilson   (Playwright/Poet)

LeRoy Carroll   (Writing, "Getting Older")

Maesoa & Walter Darton   (Support & Inspiration)

Joseph "Joe" Hall   (Everyone's Policeman)
    (Co-Chaplin)

AuthorHouse   (Guidance/Assistance)

Family & Friends

Thanks, Rick

In Memory of Our Grandson

JERRIS CERONE WILLIAMS
(RIFIKKI)

SPECIAL THANKS

To

Michael "Hap" O'Daniel
Mentor and very special friend

The best, Rick

Notes:

Stupidity qualified me to write this book.
What stupidity qualifies you to read it?

Special thanks to my buddies who
stopped by from time to time
to help me edit and proof this book.
Jack Daniel, Johnny Walker, Jim Bean, Jose Cuervo,
even Mr. Wakki Tobakki stopped to help.

At times I even saw a "Grey Goose" hovering above.

My last writing,
except to family and friends.

Again, love & thanks to my very lovely wife GWEN.
Without her this book would not
have been written.

Best, Rik

ABOUT THE BOOK

WHO SAID THAT
Bits & Pieces
Writings from an empty room
(views from my window)

It was quite a task deciding on a title for this no sense, nonsense, makes no sense compiled literature over the past years. I decided on this simple title. Because of my attraction to quotations, to quips, witticisms; ad lib one liners, etc. Whatever was said or by circumstance read I stored them in the back of my mind. I jotted them down on whatever napkin, receipt or piece of paper that was handy. This came about during social conversations with friends, relatives, celebrities, politicians, whomever. Some are mere questions, some are in fact excerpts from my first book. "I don't understand." Credit was given to those I could. Not being aware of their "Off the Cuff" statements they bounced off my head as being funny, impactful, noteworthy, stupid or tone fully intellectual. I modified, twisted or extended most of them to my mindset as I was writing. For the most part all are my original quotes/writings and poems.

If I were a baker I would describe my book as:
1 cup of wisdom
½ cup of knowledge
1 ounce of thought
1 pinch of reason
1 grain of stupidity
or an
"Downside Up Cake"

BEWARE: Decipher book's Littter-8-chewer carefully!!!!
"A sam hamich and a coff a cupee"!

Pick me up, put me down, pick me up,
read me over and over again.

WRITINGS

I AM AN AMERICAN

I am too proud to be scared
I am too strong to be afraid
I am too bold to unfold
I am too respected
to be neglected
I am too powerful
to be threatened
I am too brave not to fight
'SO BRING IT ON'

Don't get religious now,
it may be too late.

Take a look, read this book,
it may charge your mind.

I may be ugly but I'm
better looking than you.

Let your conscious be your guide
which could lead to a disaster.

You can't teach an old dog new tricks
and you can't raise grown people.

I can't remember what I forgot.

If God is your co-pilot,
change seats.

With all those animals on the "ARK"
who did the housekeeping?

"Girl you look good enough to put
in a bowl of beans."
(Ernest "Puddin" Davis)

Man adores nature
Man survives by nature
Man enjoys nature
Yet man destroys nature

Being together can at times
be filled with loneliness.

You don't have to be a care giver,
just CARE.

The difference between
wisdom and knowledge;
knowledge can be lost,
wisdom is forever.

Forgetfulness is not a problem
the problem is remembering.

Some days are long
Some days are short
Both have the same amount of hours!

Follow an ugly kid home
and see, don't somebody ugly
open the door.
(Redd Foxx/Friend)

To Rick
(My Book)
John De Rosa
DREAM – CREATE – EXPLORE
I'd rather be in an empty place filled with life,
than a packed house full of empty people.
"Inspire to be Heard"

I am the virgin stone, pebble or rock
that has never been touched or thrown

I am the person that never gets tired.
That's why I'm the worker that never gets fired.

"We're building a house from the ground up."
(Response from Ann Jones)
"What in the hell else would you build it up from?"
(even a tree house is from the ground up)

A stab in the back is not as bad
as an arrow through the heart.

Time does not heal all wounds.
some fester forever.

It is more important to believe
than not to believe.

As a child it was said to me
tomorrow never comes.
As I have grown older
I realize it doesn't.

My Father
(Raymond)
"Feed the birds
Be still
Be good to one another."

My Mother
(Eloise)
"Don't let anyone ever stop you."

My Wife
(Gwen)
"Together, we got this." "Love is precious."

Upside down cake,
which side is up,
which side is down?

You don't have to speak
in a loud voice to be heard.

You just have to
say something that is meaningful.

You may hear what I speak of,
but not know what I speak of
unless you listen.

We all have "Road Rage"
but only to a degree.
Blow your horn,
curse to yourself, even
give the Finger.
Stop there, "Bang Bang".

I'm tired of hearing
"Been there, Done that."
Tell me something new or
maybe you haven't done
a Damn thing since.
(Get a Life)

"They're off the hook"
I'm glad they're not hurting anymore.
"I beg your pardon – pardon me"
Hell, I didn't know you were in prison.

They're walking around with
a half stringer of fish.
Well at least they caught some
or maybe they ran out of bait!

"Their elevator doesn't go all the way up,"
well maybe they don't want to go to the top floor.

Why do some people walk up and down the escalator?
Be still, enjoy the ride, "stupid."

Some people know how to turn lights on
but not turn them off.

"It is what it is,"
What the hell is, is?

"Do you know What?"
Maybe, what's What's last name?

"My car's broke"
I didn't know your car had any money!

"CLOUDS"

Have you ever seen vapor wrapped in a shroud
Wonder why images are wrapped in a cloud

I'm the floating wonder that you love to see
Might I be an illusion, because you can't touch me

All my images change as I travel
Those magnificent images begin to unravel

As I move slowly you observe a change
Can't do a thing about it, I'm out of your range

I see a Dolphin, I say to my friend
They see the face of an old man
A long silver beard drooping from his chin

It's as if we're drawing, what we want to see
That's why the pictures are different, between
You and me

Clouds are only vapor
colored with hues
of white pink and blue
Slivers of silver lining
as the sun beckons through

It seems as we wonder, we ask ourselves why
GOD put such beautiful clouds in the sky

Rik, 2013

"WHERE DOES LAND END?"

This is my world the city lights have gone astray
Far so ever far, far, far away

I dwell in the heart of Mother Nature
Her beauty is superb

For those who understand it's magnificence
It's a bounty we deserve

There is no more land
God has given us it's all

Like He created the seasons
Winter, Spring, Summer and Fall

I beckon to the rising
of the golden sun

The shinning of the moon
that whispers day is done

The creatures on this earth
all the wonders He has given

Are we ever thankful enough
He's the One who inspires our livin'

Dr. Richard S. Rhodes

"I walked to school uphill both ways"
Keep going to school,
you'll soon be on top of a
mountain of education.

What's the difference between a lie and a fib?
Just tell me a story!

GOLF
Gentlemen Only
Ladies Forbidden
Glad that has Changed!

FUCK
(the origin)
Not intended to be an obscene word!
Fornication Under Command of the King
For Unlawful Carnal Knowledge

Damn, we FUCKED that word up
(see addendum)

Do poor people enjoy money
more than rich people?

I'll finish this book,
if I live long enough!

I'd rather live in an empty house
than a house of disarray.

Do I love my life, do I like my life
Do I want to change my life?
Do I want to have a live?
Am I satisfied with my life?
Or must I just endure?

Peace of mind is one of
the greatest treasures in life.

A house belongs to someone else.
A HOME belongs to you.

It's better to be listening
rather than talking.

Are you a learned, schooled, educated
intellectual individual
or a curb side "Know It All?"

How do you go through the motions
of not doing anything?

What is the "Where with all?"
Where were you?
Were you with all the people in the world?

We need to be ourselves
even if we may at times be wrong.
We always need to
be our own person within ourselves!

May we ever subdue our passion
and control our anger.

Not everyone pledges allegiance
to the United States of America
some just echo the words.

"I'm stone broke."
So you've got money
but you're out of stones.

With a cat of nine tails,
You whipped me as your slave
As my blood before me
You sent to their grave

You've raped my Mother
As I lay under her bed
You tortured my Father
His wounds lay him dead

Now I'm a free man upon you I tread
I shall not rest until you are dead
And to all of those who followed you
I make the same promise
This will also come true

"It bites my soul"

Justice to you is just having fun
LIKE ALL OF THOSE HANGINGS
You feel justice was done!

I shall forever be the blood
of my Mother's womb
and of my Father's genes.

"If God awakens me
I'll do the rest."
(Kevin Bennett)

No one has been barred on account of his race
from fighting or dying for America
there are no "white" or "colored" signs
on the foxholes or graveyards of battle.
(John F. Kennedy)

The liberals can understand everything but
the people who don't understand them.
(Lenny Bruce)

Money is like a sixth sense without which
you cannot make a complete use of the other five.
(W. Somerset Maugham)

Begin at once to live and count each day
as a separate life.
(Seneca)

The longer I live, the more beautiful
life becomes.
(Frank Lloyd Wright)

The pessimist complains about the wind:
the optimist expects it to change;
the realist adjust the sails.
(William Arthur Ward)

The pessimist sees the difficulty
in every opportunity: the optimist sees
the opportunity in every difficulty.
(Lawrence Pearsall Jacks)

Wisdom is learned you can't teach it.

It's what you've learned
after you know it all that counts.
(President, Harry Truman)

Books alone don't educate you.

Best two times to go fishing are when
it's raining and when it's not.
(Fisherman's saying)

You can dislike something
yet still have the reasoning to understand why!

There' a fine line between a moron and an idiot
so fine it doesn't exist.

Why tell someone
you'll be there in a minute

and you're ten miles away,
or you're not even dressed yet!

I've had students so dumb
they didn't know the fourth letter
in the alphabet.

Don't tell me you'll fix my problems
make them go away.

I know just how you feel.
Then why aren't you crying?

Cheer up things could be worse
so I cheered up and damn it, things got worse.

Why do women wait to get in the car
to put their lipstick on?

One can be over schooled and under educated.

Confusion is when the wind
is blowing both ways at the same time.

One can count the seconds, minutes, hours, days,
even the years in life, but never the heartbeats.

Everyone has a book in their life, why not write it?

An alcoholic knows where they're going in life
a drunk doesn't even know where they've been.

Life has two rules: Number one,
Never quit! Number two, Always
remember number one.
(Duke Ellington/Musician)

Be as you are and hope that it's right.

You don't have to speak in a loud voice to be heard;
just say something that is meaningful.

Those who don't pay child support are
ASSHOLES.

Those who born a child
and not take care of the child
is not a parent they're
not just one turd,
they're a pile of shit.

You don't just grow into manhood
you have to achieve it.

Honor thy mother and father,
more important.
LOVE them.

The older you get the more
you appreciate everything.

You push me
I push you
why not just hug?
Can one be educated and
still be stupid?

Now let me tell you
So you stuck out your chest
I won this game
So I must be the best.

Why don't Black people understand
RSVP?
Because CPT isn't spelled the same way.

Interruptions are broken thoughts.

Don't get no better than this.
(Ernest Puddin' Davis)

Which is stronger, determination or will?
One is in the mind, the other in the heart!

One should explore wisdom
which creates thought.

WISDOM
I've learned more out of school
than in school.

There is a difference between
the mind, heart and soul.
(think about it)

Has a part of your body
ever left you overnight?
Those aches and pains in the morning!

One of a kind, kind of what?

One picture is worth a thousand words,
some only worth a few.

I am an optimist; it doesn't seem too much use
being anything else.

In the wilderness is the salvation of mankind.
(Henry David Thoreau)

We can never have enough of nature.
(Henry David Thoreau)

Nature is the art of God.
(Dante)

Patience is power.
(Chinese Proverb)

Never cut what you can untie.
(Joseph Joubert)

Patience is the companion of wisdom.
(St. Agustine)

One should spread wisdom,
it creates thought.

You crack me up
you're concrete
that's been pounded.

To some people TV is more important than life,
to others it is their life, includes video games.

Most scholars spread knowledge
few spread ignorance.

Did the house burn up or
did it burn down?

As I see it, how many others do?
Religion and politics
neither of which has any solidarity.

Some people can't chew gum
and walk at the same time.

Shut up – Shut down!

(Someone you haven't seen in decades)
Do you know who I am?
If you don't know why are you asking me?

You get out of it
what you put in to it.
"Where's all my
slot machine money?"

When all is said and done
may your life become
a long letter rather than
a short note.

I didn't understand an older friend telling me,
they don't drive at night anymore!
I understand now, I've had another birthday.

To live in a vacuum means
you're collecting dirt.

So you have a degree,
do something with it!

Some people know everything about one thing
and nothing about anything else.

Saving money doesn't mean anything
unless you start today.

A one tract mind is one of life's enormous deficiencies.

He who lives in a vacuum breathes none of life's clean air.

Money
"I want to be a "1099" rather than a "W2."
(Steven A. Smith)
Sport analysis

One fifth of the people are against everything
all of the time.
(Robert Kennedy)

I beg your pardon
I didn't know you were in prison!

They're off the hook.
Glad they're not hurting anymore.
They're off the chain, which gang were they on?

"It's Chili Time"
(ANYTIME)

Injustice resilient, the truth never sleeps
(Leonard Pitts)
Reporter, Miami Hearld
Ferguson unrest, 2015

The great mistake is believing you're
intelligent when you're not.

To live in a vacuum means you don't need
a sweeper.

Aging
Has your body ever left you at night,
those aches and pains in the morning.

While interviewing a client!
"Do you feel me?"
"Hell no, I haven't touched you."
(Jerry Brower)
A Chemical Dependent Counselor

Most things aren't learned from a distance.

You have to learn how
to be nasty nicely.
(Heather Britton)

Some things on TV insult my intelligence,
others praise my stupidity.

Some people enjoy the moment,
others don't realize it was ever here.

"Ain't over until the fat lady sings."
Find a skinny lady and get the show over.

Some things have a reason,
others have a purpose.

The only things we care about
are the things we understand.

Do you want anything or not?
I don't want anything, bring me some not.

People who talk to themselves
have a problem thinking.

I'm thinking to myself,
who else can you think to?

A good moonshiner drives the car backward
as fast as forward.

How do you think out loud?

"Hey, what's up?"
The clouds, the sky.

"Hey, what if justice should always prevail over injustice:
We shall forever be a nation content.
(unrealistic)

With seconds to play before the game is over,
who's side is GOD on, yours or mine?
Does GOD choose sides?

I'd rather go to bed early and get up early,
than go to bed late and can't get up.
The early bird gets the worm,
the late one gets the sleep.
(unkown)

Financially, I'm set for life,
if I don't have to buy anything.
(Denny)

"Brownsville Boys"
I've been to Brownsville Texas,
so hot a place I'd never want to live.
I could only remember the "Brownsville Boys".
Their innocent lives they unjustly had to give.
I remember, there, my heart was filled
with anger and sorrow.
My only solitude was I knew,
I was leaving Brownsville tomorrow.
(see addendum)

It Bites My Soul

A rolling stone gathers no moss
but it's destine to cause a crash.

God didn't make any more land,
why destroy what we have?

The task is always perceived to be
quick and easy.
Halfway through taking it on
it's "Oh shit what the hell."

"AN ISLAND"

"Hey Mon" I'm on the happy island
The mountains and the sea
The taste of ake and sailfish
The steel drums callin' me

Rhythmically they think and tong
To the Reggae sound
There is no more joyful music
Anywhere around

Chrystal waters enhanced
With brightness of green and blue
Swallowed between the mountains
As the capture you

The natives whitest teeth sparkle
In contrast to their shiny black skin
The most beautiful people
Of any place I've ever been

Every time they greet you
There is a smile upon their face
You ask yourself and wonder
Why it's not like this every place

What's this island called
People ask of me
JAMAICA is its name
You have to go and see

Rick Rhodes

IT IS THE SOLDIER-

It is the soldier, not the reporter,
Who has given us freedom of the press
It is the soldier, not the poet
Who has given us freedom of speech
It is the soldier, not the campus organize
Who has given us the right to a fair trial
I is the soldier, not, not the pastor,
who has given us the right to worship
It is the soldier, nota the politician,
Who has given us the right to vote
It is the soldier, not the media,
The right to take a knee
who has given the dissenter
as our National Anthem we sing
to sit out the pledge
of allegiance to our flag
It is the soldier, who salutes the flag
serves the flag, serves under the flag
and whose coffin is draped
by the flag, who gives the protester
the right to burn the flag
(unknown)

Hope for more
be grateful for less.

Love has a blessing
hate needs a lesson.

A chip off the old block,
your father was a square.

Lose the battle but win the war.

How long is an instant?

Education is a paper key,
it opens the door to success.

To errr is human
to forgive is a virtue.

It's not a matter who you know,
it's a matter of who you are.

At my age if it doesn't have a banister
I'm not climbing it!

Birds don't have cell phones,
but they call each other.

"What goes around comes around"
Boy I wish I hadn't kicked
that kid's ass yesterday!

"I agree to disagree"
What the hell does that mean?

No one is ugly
they're just not good looking!
Then what are they?

"Counting sheep will put you to sleep."
Are there any sheep in your bedroom?

Why does envy always have to be green?

EASTER
Chickens go on strike so bunnies can lay colored Easter eggs.

I am Black
I am Mulatto
No matter what you think my face is
I'm born the child of many bloods,
lands, tribes and races
I am Mulatto
I am Proud

I can impart truth
I can impart knowledge
I can impart wisdom
however
only you can obtain it.

The bigger they are
the harder they
have to fall.
(Robert Fitzsimmons)

Don't care about what I'm doing,
care about how I am.

Talk to me about something
other than yourself.

Why is Cincinnati airport in Kentucky?
Dallas airport isn't in New Mexico!

Black lives matter
so do White lives
ALL lives matter.

The act of bravery
was embedded
in the womb.

Life can't do it alone
it's not a givin',
you have to face the
challenges to keep on livin'.

I'm the person that can't sing in the shower, if
you can't sing, you can't sing. There's a law
against making "Loud Noise."

It matters not how bad you lose,
It's how often you lose.

"WINDOW SHOPPING"
When you break the glass
and take what you want.

Not only respect your elders, respect everyone.

Matter of fact, FACTS do matter.

"GOOD TROUBLE"
(Congressman John Louis)

Teach yourself to never have
a non-productive day.

"Kids should be seen not heard."
That's what makes some
adults stupid.

One thing I learned out of school,
is how to play "Hooky."

If your parachute doesn't open,
damn the rip cord
"CLOSE YOUR EYES."

The longer you shower, the more
body oils you lose.

Don't march to the beat of the drum,
march to your heartbeat.

Watch where you step
it could be on yourself.

Sometimes we need to slap ourselves, Hard!
If a "Genie" ever grants you one wish;
wish for three more then you won't
waste one.

Everyone has a number on their back, the only
one that sees it is the ALMIGHTY.

"Takes one to know one!"
I want to know more than one.

They say! "Old people could make
something out of nothing."
I want to know what ingredient
they put in nothing?

You are BRAVER than you believe
STRONGER than you seem and
SMARTER than you think.
(unknown)

(Moron going out the door)
Idiot: "Where you going?"
Moron: "Nowhere."
Idiot: "Well call me when you get there."

World's dumbest firing squad,
they stand in a circle.

SANCTIONS are paper bullets.

What goes up must come down!
TAXES Hah-hah

Take away Putin's brush
so he can stop painting us yellow.

New York directions
"Straight ahead!"

FYI
The human femur bone can support 30
times the weight of a person's body.
Ounce for ounce, that's stronger than steel.

No matter where you drop it,
it never falls where you can find it.

It's as cold as a well digger's ass.
Then the devil must be wearing long johns.

"Gas is as high as a giraffe's ass."
(Walter Darton)

What is a "Third World Country?"
As I see it, there's only one world!

"My bodyguard Rick has a karate jump kick
so high he reads the newspaper before
he comes down."
(Redd Foxx/Friend)

"Little boy Blue go blow your horn,
he'll break his neck trying to blow
his HORN."
(Redd Foxx/Friend)

You cannot mend a broken heart
but you can redeem a lost soul.

When the Lord comes to take
me away I wish I could say,
hold on Lord, I got a few
more chapters to read."
(Joe Hall)
(Policeman, Co-Chaplin)

"Only God can walk on water, we
have to find the stones."
(Joe Hall)
(Policeman, Co-Chaplin)

"Love, Peace, Respect and Power to UKRAINE."

"I asked my shrink, what's the best way for
me to commit suicide?" He said, "Take a gun
and shoot yourself under your left breast."
"I did and blew my damn kneecap off."
(Moms Mabley/Comedian, Friend)

I asked my cousin Reggie since his retirement:
what it's like being home with his wife Gwen
all day, everyday? He said, "We're in the choking
stage right now."
(Reggie Camp)

"Life's Life"

Life is a reality you can't fake it
It's your charge you have to make it
Step by step your journey begins
Be strong have faith see it until it ends
The long road ahead you have to travel
There'll be decisions you'll have to unravel
Step by step you're all alone
The task is yours you're on your own
I think to myself what must I do
Have faith be strong and see it through
Now that those trials and hardships
have departed
I look back with pride from whence
I first started
I have a vision of a wonderful future I see
I now have faith I have peace of mind
I'm in control of my life's destiny
As I travel forward from season to season
I understand everyone's life was put
here for a reason
Though some of my dreams have been
torn and shattered
Through faith courage and love
in my heart I shall ever cherish
only those that have mattered
As I sit alone musing to this very day
There's a pride and a comfort
because I traveled my way

Rik

"REDNECK"

Praise to the Redneck
for he is our hero
He is the person that
makes sure our vegetables grow
Up in the morning crack of dawn
out in the fields till daylight has gone

Pride to his overalls though
tattered, weathered and torn
Proud to be a farmer since the day
he was born
Spends the whole day in the
mid summer's heat
Sun beaming on the
back of his neck slowly
turning it as red as a beet

His whole body racked with
pain growing old
Still he won't quit till
he plants his last row

Thanks to the Redneck for
all of his giving
He furnishes the nourishment
that keeps us all living

Rik

If you don't know your history, you don't
know where to go with your future.
(Rev. Al Sharpton)

Marriage!
Why buy the cow when you're getting
the milk free?

Good House Keeping,
If you don't like it, use it or want it,
don't clean it, pitch It.

At times cursing is therapy
for the soul.

Forcing yourself to smile
won't make you feel better.

Is wearing your heart on your sleeve
a fashion statement or does it just
give your heart a breath of fresh air?

Is two for one better than
twice as big?

If you're a nut, you're
edible, not crazy.

TV watching or finger exercising
won't make you productive.

Throw something away today you don't
really like. It's called
"Soul Cleansing."

Army Saying
"Your as is grass and I'm the lawnmower."

Be nosey in the kitchen and
watchful in the world.

"How many times have I told you?"
I don't know, I haven't been counting.

What you say is not as
important as what you do.
(Rev. Al Sharpton)

Ron and Ann at their neighbor's party,
having too much fun and too much
goat's milk. Leaving the party, Ann asked Ron,
"Who's driving?" They only live next door.

You may fool all of the people some of the time;
You can even fool some of the people all the
Time; but you can't fool all the people all the time.
(Abraham Lincoln)

It is not best to swap horses
when crossing streams.
(Abraham Lincoln)

"Oh, bye the way."
What the hell does that mean?
What way?

Why live in a shell if you're not a turtle?

Don't cry on my shoulder,
cry in my arms.

Why do I have a headache every Sunday morning?
Oh boy, those Saturday nights.

I can't wait until tomorrow because
I get better looking every day.
(Joe Namath/ football/Hall of Fame)

Some people just don't understand.
"Tomorrow Never Comes."

You'll never have an ending
unless you have a beginning.

The only guys that have filthy underwear
are the ones that show them.
Cover your asshole.
"ASSHOLE"

The right way, the wrong way,
The ARMY WAY

Some people acquire beautiful real estate
and turn it into a "Section Eight."

Sometimes Cupid's arrow misses its mark.

Why do people cut holes in a pair of good jeans?
Guess it's so their knees can get a breath of fresh air.

Why does my GPS keep getting me lost?

Give me my roses while I'm alive.
Hell, you don't deserve any,
"Dead or Alive."
(Who said that?)

Keep on keeping on!
No,
Keep on holding on.

Smorgasboard
Aman is invited for dinner.
"Darn rick, all this food, I'm on a diet."
"What kind of diet." "A 'C' food diet." "You
can only eat C food." "No, the more food I
see, the more I eat."
(Arman Hastoyan/Friend)

We bought Arman a gift, a shirt, it was too small.
I told him I would exchange it. He said, "No Rick,
I could have worn it last month but not this month,
so I'll wear it off and on."
(Arman Hastoyan)

Interview
That's a good question, hold it.
Give me a good answer, asshole,
hold it.
Where, (In our hands)

"I'd rather you stick me in my arm
than stick me in the ground."
(Dusty Rhodes/my Son)

Checkers are played with the hand
chess is played with the mind.

Why do students carry school books home
and never open them?

Why carry a back pack filled with toilet paper
or an empty briefcase
with only a lunch meat sandwich?
Is this a fashion statement, or an ego trip?

Make the short money first
you'll never get rich quick.

"It's raining cats and dogs!"
Why not snakes and alligators?
Down SOUTH it's raining,
"Pitch forks and Nigger babies."
Let us all have the same weather!

"He's walking around with a half stringer of fish."
Maybe he ran out of bait.

Don't stop, you're on a roll.
Get me off, I don't like sweets.

If you drive too fast, you'll get there too soon.

"They can't walk and chew gum at the same time."
Pat your head and rub your stomach at the same time.
(Now switch)

"Hey man, what's up? The clouds and the sky."

Most things aren't learned from a distance!

Comedians are human.

Beat them up, no, beat them down.

If you have to hurry to get some place
you're already late.

KNOWLEDGE
Those who want to know
Those who don't care to know
Those who think they know
Those who know
Those who think they
know it all!
Witch am I?

"Come on man!"
Where you going?

I told you so, I knew
so, you said so, so what.
What the hell is so?

Do whatever you have to do
Do whatever you want to do
Do whatever you need to do
Do whatever you're going to do
Don't wait, just do it

It takes strength and courage
to become your own person.

If heaven is just a step away, take a broad jump.

Rink, circle field,
course or court
the riches sport in the world
is played on a DIAMOND

A professor on their way to class
"Let me go spread some ignorance."

Doing nothing is the same as
not doing anything.

The older you get
the fewer colds you catch and
the more funerals you attend.

"Rick, why didn't I see you at the funeral?"
"Because I'm not dead yet."

Twenty four of our Presidents were first born,
eight were left handed.

The difference between
a fib, a lie and a story is
who you're telling it to and why.

It's one thing to lose, it's
another to beat yourself.

DREAMS, DELUSIONS, ILLUSIONS and REALITY
Learn to differentiate, one from the other
(Delusions of grandeur)

Some people enjoy the moment,
Some take advantage of the moment,
Others don't realize it was ever here

Do people who talk to themselves aloud
hear someone on the other end?

Hey, what's up? The sky, clouds
and don't forget the astronauts;
space ships along with
the other junk we've sent up there.

"I'm Damned if I do, damned if I don't"
Well don't do either, just stick your thumb
up your butt and breath.

You know I taught you better than that.
Then why do they keep doing it?

If the teacher fails to teach
the student fails to learn.
(Every ones a teacher)

Your church is where you worship.
Your home is where you live.
You can only worship in your church.
However, you can live and worship
in your home.

Doctors Visit
Went for my check-up!
"Redd, if you want to live, the best thing you
can do; give up smoking, drinking,
partying and sex."
"Doc, I can't do the best thing

what's the next best?"
(Redd Foxx/friend/ comedian)

(There's that T after the X again!)

Does not going to church
send you on a guilt trip?

What does crossing your fingers
really mean?
Not a damn thing.
Why not just cross your legs?

Standing in the doorway.
"OK, I'm gone."
Why do I still see you?

I'll be there in a minute to pick you up.
Do you know how much I weigh?

Don't just give it up, use it up!
(Audrey/old friend)

"I'm dead broke."
"Well, now you don't
need to buy anything."
Treat your pets with love, you'll be rewarded.

"What's your dog's name?"
"Ginger."
Does Ginger Bite?"
"No, Ginger snaps."

When will you be home?
Whenever I'm there.

Why are some smart people, stupid?

"A bird in the hand is worth two in the bush."
What?

Why do people like to skate backwards?"
They can't see where they're going.

Would you rather hear help is
on the way;
or rescue is on the way?
Help can help you do the dishes.
Rescue can keep you from
doing the dishes.

I've caught a cold.
How fast was it running?

Don't do what you want to do
before doing what you need to do.

REMINDER in Mail
"This is your last chance!"
Good, I don't like to take chances.

My nose is running.
Well go catch it.

How do you separate something
that's not put together?

Sometimes the task is small
Sometimes the task is large
Success depends on
the person that's in charge.

Always do what you need to do
Before you do what you want to do
You'll never have the problem
of what you have to do.

Having Lunch
"Give me a bite,
ouch, that hurt."

How high is up?
Once the width and
twice the height.
"Hell I don't know."

Stop reaching for the stars
your arms won't get any longer.

DON'T LET ME DIE TOMORROW

Lord don't let me die tomorrow

I'm not finished with what I have to say

Lord don't let me die tomorrow

Give me more time to pray

It was you that gave me the gift of preaching

I need more time to keep on teaching

Lord give me just one more day

I have to let the world know   English

Love, peace and freedom is a better way

Then when you tap me on my shoulder

I won't hesitate, I'm on my way

LAWDY Jesus don't let me die t'morrer

Not finished wit what I's gotta say

Oh please LAWDY Jesus don't let me die t'morrer

I needs mo time ta pray

T'was You dat gave me dat gift of preachin'

Please don't let me die ta'morra I's needs mo time

To keep on teachin '4   Slave

Gotta let all dee peoples know

Freedom, love and peace is de better way

Den when you taps me on my shoulder

Won't hesitate, I's on my way   Rick, 2020

"DEAD BROKE"

Landlord called
did you pay the rent
How could I
Ain't got one damn cent
Well did you put gas in the car?
Can't get to the pump,
Won't make it that far
Well did you pay the electric bill?
That's the money we borrowed,
sent it to Fanny and Will
You tellin' me we broke,
Ain't got no money
We in front of a rock
Pushin' a boulder honey
Well we have to pawn
my wedding ring
Done tried that, ain't worth
a damn thing
Gotta find a way to get
outa this rut
Go find a job, get off
your butt
Think you gonna live off
my welfare money
Ain't gonna happen got news
for you honey
I'm tired of livin' through
all this hell
Spent my part time money
to raise your bail
Ain't done a damn thing
Since you got outa jail
"PACK UP YOUR SHIT
AND HIT THE TRAIL"   (Rick, 2022)

My last check was like a football,
it bounced every which a way.
(By the way, where is every witch and every way?)

The King's English is all fucked up, let's try the Queen's!

I am the child of my Mother's womb
and forever I shall stay within her.

Birthdays don't mean anything
unless you're old or you're young.

You don't have to be on the same page;
as long as you're reading the same book.

As it pains our hearts to know
we were bought and sold.
But in our soul we knew
we were worth more than the
White man's gold.
The time of slavery must
come to an ending
but as Negroes our sorrow
and pains never mending

"IT HAPPENED"

"It bites my soul"

It was a memorable three days
I spent with Mohammed Ali.

"You're late." "So what?"

"Off the cuff." Didn't know you were
on my sleeve.

Love the vision of special faces
when you're all alone.

"Takes two to tango," no partner,
dance by yourself.

"Go fly a kite!" It's not March yet.

The difference between a survivor
and achiever is,
a survivor remains stagnant
an achiever moves forward.

A caretaker takes care of nature.
A caregiver takes care of people.

"Be careful, not carefree."
(Dr. Shaffner)

It's easier to wear a mask than a ventilator.

"Stress is never final, failure is never total,
it's courage that counts."
(John Wooden/Basketball Coach)

The lack of reading, lends to the
absence of knowledge.

You learn more out of school than in school.
Academics may fade, life's lessons are forever.

Grass is always greener
on the other side of the fence
because its cared for.

"Have a good day," rather say, "Have a good life."

"Have a good one" I want more than one!

"It ain't cheatin' unless you get caught."
(Dolly Pardon)

Make the short money first
you'll never get rich quick.

Inform males that won't get VAXED
it's laced with "Viagra"
watch the supply run out!!!!

"If a girl knows the ropes
she'll never get tied up."
(Mae West)

"He who is not courageous enough to take
risk in life will accomplish nothing in life."
(Muhammad Ali)

"If you can back it up, it's not bragging."
(Muhammad Ali)

"A sam hammich and a coff of cupee."
(George Duke Wilson/Artist)

Can you eat and drink backwards?
My wife taking a shot of Tequila.
First, a lick of salt a taste of lemon
then the Tequila!
"Gwen are you trying to get drunk backwards?"

Taking the shortcut means
you missed something.

The inevitable, except it.

If you can dream it,
you can achieve it.

I'm never late, I'm just not on time.

You can't write it, you can't paint it
unless you feel it.

"CPA", Constant Pain in the Ass.

Need vs. Greed

The younger you ask questions
the more you learn.

Don't put your shoes on before your socks.

"Don't count the days
make the days count."
(Mohammad Ali)

(Broken glass)
You can recover some of the pieces
but you can never recover all of them.

Learn to see…listen…and think for yourself.
(Malcolm X)

It doesn't matter how high up you are
unless you are falling.

A one track mind is usually
headed for a collision.

There are three sides to every story,
two lies and the truth.

Tell it like it is or
tell it like you want it to be.

Opinions are like assholes
everybody has one.

We all have
beliefs, morals, values and
attitudes, it makes us who we are.

Why get a tattoo
where you can't even see it?
Why give a child a name you can pronounce
but can't spell?

It's not how young you look
it's how old you are.

Do something a little special each day
then reward yourself.

Is there a difference between
wisdom and wit?
(Griswell Freeman)

Education is hanging on
until you've caught on.
(Robert Frost)

The first rule of business
is to mind your own.

Worry not about the words of your enemies
but beware the silence of your friends.

Wisdom is the breath of life
don't be selfish share it.

Does coffee taste better
in your favorite cup?

Does wine taste better
in a wine glass?

The pessimist complains about the wind;
the optimist expects it to change;
the realist adjust the sails.
(William Arthur Ward)

"I'm still learning."
Michael Angelo's Motto

I am an optimist it does seem too much
use being anything else.
(Winston Churchill)

Optimism is the faith that leads
to achievement. Nothing can be done
without hope and confidence.
(Helen Keller)

Borderline
I use to wonder
About living and dying –
I think the difference lies
Between tears and crying

I use to wonder
About here and there –
I think the distance
Is nowhere
(Langston Hughes)

Justice is not only blind
it's also cripple.

Rick or Rik
Depends on who I am at the time!

Melvin Slappy White's

BROTHERHOOD CREED

If the White man
And the Black man
Would work hand and hand
We could make this world a promised land
You've got George Washington
We've got Booker T.
You've got congressmen in congress
And so have we
Einstein split the atom, no ifs, ands or but
Look what Dr. Carver did with a little peanut
We will forget about slavery
You forget the Indian raids
We quit calling you ofays
And you quit calling us spades
Together we will wipe out poverty and hate
And we will conquer outer space
So why don't we just get together
And let all of us share God's grace

(Slappy/Comedian/Friend)
Prepared by the Whitehouse of Slappy White

(signed, To Rick from Slappy)
(see addendum)

I'm gonna go down south,
find (Jim Crow) and
kick his ass.

So help me God, damn it
help yourself.

Why ask God for help
when you don't need it?

God Doesn't
Run touchdowns, hit homeruns, shoot
three pointers, win or lose games, choose
sides, or even bet! You do that on your own.

The country's going to hell
in a handbag.
What country can fit
into a handbag?

"Well Anyway"
What?

"Rick, don't quit, keep writing."
"I can't, I'm out of vodka."

Why can't you get on a horse
from either side?

He likes to sleep on his side,
bury him that way.

Discussing food I asked my friend Karl.
Have you ever eaten bear meat?

Response: "I don't eat anything
that can eat me."

In my heart and in my mind,
I'll always have fond memories
of those that are left behind.

Real gas vs. Human gas
a matter of economics.

Do bunnies really lay Easter eggs?

Do we have ten fingers or
eight fingers and two thumb,
how about eight footies and two toes?

"You've got me up a tree."
"No, you got your ass up there."

Let us never negotiate out of fear,
but let us never fear to negotiate
(John Fitzgerald Kennedy)

Mankind must put an end to war
or war will put an end to mankind.
(unknown)

When time is of the essence
take a deep breath.

Always remember!
"EMMIT TILL"

In desperation,
I became desperate
"Bang."

Jack and Jill went up the hill
to get a pail of water
"Hell water doesn't run uphill
I know what they went up there for."
(Redd Foxx/Friend)

The difficult we do immediately.
The impossible takes a little longer.

Good Advice
is not always good.

No one can think and talk
at the same time.

If the heart is soft,
how can it be broken?

"Bottoms Up"
Are you drinking
or mooning?

Do fat people skinny dip?

The older the relationship
the more pecks on the cheek.
Damn I miss those kisses.

Why do females have a more
attractive handwriting than males?

Legends are created,
Heroes are born.

How do you look up to someone
shorter than you?

What would life be like if we
became younger each day?

(Old Age)
Don't count the birthdays
feel the warning signs.

Some people are so lazy they won't get up
to get the remote.

You can lose the battle
and still win the war.

It takes courage to speak loud and freely
without having fear.
Than be quite or speak softly
about what others want to hear.

Sometime we should do ourselves
a favor, "Shut-Up."

Is behavior learned or taught? Wake up parents!

When it's cold to one
it's not cold to another.
When it's hot it's hot
to everybody.

MY OWN PERSON

I'm my own person
whether young or old
I'm my own person
I'm the one in control

I'm my own person
You don't tell me what to do
I say to myself,
who the hell are you?

I'm my own person
I control my destiny
Only the Lord dictates
the decisions inside of me

I'm my own person
I make my own decisions
You don't have to understand
my reasons or my visions

I'm my own person
I know exactly where I'm going
Being my own person
helps me carry on

If I make a mistake
which causes grief or sorrow
Being the person that I am
I'll take care of it tomorrow

If that precious voice whispers
this is your final day
Being my own person
I'll find my own way

Dr. Rick Rhodes

TIME

How the year passed

It's come to an ending

Had things to do

Never got mending

Said "Tomorrow I'll get around to it."

Time passed so fast

I just didn't do it

As time passes by

Age is getting us down

Stay in one place

Just don't get around

All of those friends

We love so much

Think of them daily

But don't stay in touch

As we vision the horizon

Of the oncoming year

Give thanks to our LORD

That we are still here

Dr. Rick Rhodes

God has nothing to do with it,
if you can believe it,
you can achieve it.

I don't over eat,
I'm over fed.

Lord, God, Allah, Almighty, Buddha,
Supreme Being, Satin, Devil.
Confusing to me!

Pray sometime without
asking for anything.

To be lucky is one thing.
To be blessed is another.

"Sudden Death" on the golf course,
Did someone die?
Stroke!!!

Why do we look down to pray?
Does God want to see the back
of our heads?

Why is it called the "World Series of Baseball?"
Are we pitching a "Shut Out?" No other countries
are involved.

Some people ask God for everything
and never attend church.

(My neighbor, Ron Jones)
"Hey Rick, Ann's got a new job."
"Oh yeah, what's she doing?"
"Working in the in the new weed plant,
"Great Ron."
Ron's wife is a retired State Trooper

Hope is the pebble that keeps you going.
Prayer is the rock that carries you on.

A Pretty Woman has a lovely face.
A Beautiful Lady
has the gift of grace.

(Kentucky – known for)
"Good whisky, pretty women
and fast horses."
Also
"Good whisky, pretty horses
and fast women."

A home without humor
is like doing jail time.

Those who are not willing to read
are punishing themselves.

To all of those men who can
put the toilet seat up
but can't put it down.
(Show some respect)

There are lawmakers and false lawmakers.
Some are Americans, some are false Americans.

Humpty Dumpty sat on the wall,
Humpty Dumpty had a great fall.
All the king's horses and
all the king's men,
couldn't put Humpty together again,
(Ever dropped a raw egg on the floor?)
Horses can't put anything together!

"Little Red Riding Hood."
What was she riding and was Hood
her real last name?

Some people are saying out loud now,
what they use to whisper.
You know who they are.
(Rev. Al Sharpton)

"A penny for your thoughts."
My thoughts don't come that cheap.

My wife ask me, "Rick, have you lost your mind?"
I ask her, "Can you lose your mind more than once?"

"A hard head makes a soft behind."
(Correction)
A hard head makes a sore behind.

You don't have to have a birthday
to get older, we get older every day.

I'm on my way to pick you up.
Do you know how much I weigh?

PARACHUTE
(First & last Jump)
"I will never, never, ever jump from another
airplane. The plane was going three times faster
than it was suppose too. My whole life passed
in front of me and the ground was so far, far down."
"UN-BELIEVE-ABLE."
Lincoln Ware
(Radio/TV talk show host)

Lincoln, if your whole life passed in front of you,
you'd still be falling! (Smile) From one jumper
to another, welcome to an elite club, I love it.
RIK

Police Officer: "Call me PIG,"
I'm Proud, PRIDE, INTEGRITY & GUTS.

Don't let people put words into
your mouth, do that yourself.

Don't be afraid to speak
what you believe, have courage.

The truth never sleeps.

Have you awakened in the morning
and felt like your body had three
birthdays overnight?
Have you ever awakened in the
morning, gotten dressed and
realized it's your day off?
"Oh boy, what a night!"

Racism begets anger at the same
time it can instill PRIDE.

REALIZEATION:
Today, kids teach their parents.
(Math, Arithmetic)

Curiosity never killed any cat,
be curious not nosey.

Feed the birds,
their songs are free.
They make joyful sounds
for you and me.

To my wife
(New Year resolution)
"2022"
There will be no bad days,
some days will just not
be as good as others!

(A friend asked me)
What's the difference between
sky diving vs. scuba diving?
Sky diving, exhilarating.
Scuba diving, adventurous.

Why does time always go by
faster than you want; when
you have something to do?

The moron found out most accidents happen
within three miles of your home, so he moved.

"Wake up America"
Someone said it.
I'll say it again!
If we don't wake up
we won't win.

You can never catch up on
lost sleep.

Call a friend today neither one of you
may not be here tomorrow.

"Where you when all HELL broke loose?"
"Above ground."

My wife Gwen reminded me
I use to have the energy of a
12 volt battery now I've become
a slow leaking flat tire.

Reverend Ril Beatty
(My wife's cousin)
After delivering one of his
dynamic eulogies, I said, "Rev, I don't
want you to preach at my funeral.
With a puzzled look he retorted, "Why not
Rick?" I said "Because then, I wouldn't
be able to come to yours."

Sometimes you have to
lose yourself to find
yourself.

Life is the canvas upon
which you paint your life.

Some things come easy,
some things come hard.
Except both!

After all these years
I still have GWEN-i'tis

"Do you read me brother?"
"You don't look like a book to me."

Gifts from a President
A president that gave you
a horse without a saddle
a canoe without a paddle
reptiles from the swamp.
Jail birds and criminals
took away the gift of
"Make America Great Again"
with lies, corruption and deceit
taught us to Hate Again
destroying our DEMOCRACY.

The lazy riser is the
non achiever.

To be successful, travel in
one direction.
No sense in starting
over and over again.

SLEEPYHEAD

Don't hear that alarm a' ringing
Birds outside chirping and singing

Lord giving you a beautiful day
You lying there, eyes closed
sleeping it away

Pulling those covers up
over your head
Pretending you haven't heard
a word I've said

You know you got plenty
work to do
Aint nobody going to do
it for you

Staying up, party all night
don't want to enjoy
the broad daylight

Now darkness lingers
the daylight is gone
Keep your eyes closed
as you sleep on

You have not responded
to what has been said
Now sleep on forever,
know what it's like to be dead

Rik

"OLE FRIENDS"

Cherish ole friends as they grow a few
They're the greatest people that one ever knew

Be fond of old memories as you travel on
Greet new friends the long time ones are gone

You remember their faces as time passes by
Then as you wonder you ask yourself why?

Slowly you realize as you're growing old
In a matter of time you'll fit the same mold

Suddenly it becomes of you the knowledge you've found
In silence you count your fingers not too many left around

You fall asleep at night to face another day
Awaken to the morning to find one more has passed away

By Dr. Richard S. Rhodes 2012

If you start late you'll finish late
or won't finish at all.

As time goes by
staying in touch
lifts one's spirits
gives feelings of joy
it means so much.

No wonder you're bored you're lazy.

Gossip is only good
if it's bad.

They think their God's gift,
in fact they're
really a return item.

"She thinks she's all that
and a Bag of Chips!"

"Once upon a time!"
How do you get upon a time?

"Bouquet of Flowers"
(From Kip Price)
Happiness keeps you Sweet
Trials keep you Strong
Sorrows keep you Human
Failures keep you Humble
Success keeps you Glowing
But…Only Friends
Keep You Going!
"Thanks Kip"

While sitting comfortably why
is everything you want
just out of reach?

Do you know your ABC's?
There's only one "C" in the alphabet.
Why add the "S"?
Why do we spell it, leaving half
of the letters off?

Don't put your shoes on
before your socks.

Everybody's going to die, but
everybody's not going to heaven.

I write because I feel it
I write because I'm free
I write because it lets out
what's inside of me.

I paint because I feel it
I paint because I'm free
I create the hues of colors
that others want to see.

Sometimes words put on paper
speak louder than mouth to ear.

Others may encourage you, however,
you must be your own inspiration.

There are times we should put on paper
what we feel in our hearts.
"Put your thinking cap on."
If your cap has to think for you,
you're in deep shit.

The best writings are not what
you want to publish,
but what you want to share.

True authors don't write for money,
they write because of need.

People that live in the "Bible Belt" at times
miss a loop in their trousers.

Have you ever seen bugs on Bunny?

Are Robin Hood and Little Red Riding Hood related;
what was she riding?

How tall do you have to be, not to be short?

Some of us have sense
Some of us have nonsense
Some of us have no sense

You can't tell a book by its cover, so read it.

Ah, but a man's reach should exceed his grasp.
Or what's a heaven for.
(Robert Browning/Poet)
a favorite

"Chicken Little" wasn't wrong
he was just ahead of his song.
Years ago we heard him callin'
look out people the sky's a fallin'
We put all that junk up there
now it's fall 'in everywhere.
(Look up and look out, shit flies)

"Never look a gift horse in the mouth"
Would someone please tell me what that means?

What goes up must come down.
SMOKE!

Why do some people put rings in their nose
and lips and don't belong to any tribe.

Records are made to be broken,
even the worst ones.

My wife asks me, "Rick, have you lost your mind?"
I ask her, "Can you lose your mind more than once?"

Prayer is the power of belief.
Crossing fingers is the power of hope.
Leave it to the ALMIGHTY to
do His work.

Pray for others rather than yourself.

I am dying from the help of too many physicians.
(Alexander the Great)

"A DREAM VANISHED"

A beautiful bird is in your hand
Suddenly it fly's away
You know you'll never see it again
No not another day

A very special part of life
Is snatched away from you
You silently sit and ponder
Dear Lord what must I do

This special dream disappears
Which causes so much pain
You make yourself a promise
You'll never dream again

Is this an aberration
Will it make me stronger
Will it last forever
Or even last much longer.

Dr. Richard "Rick" Rhodes

"LONELY"

What's it like to sit alone
When everyone has gone
Somehow you find a thread of strength
Which helps you carry on

You feel that you are suffocating
The air's a grayish gloom
You realize there is no key
To escape the darkness of this room

All the world has abandoned you
You're the one that's left behind
Particles of despair penetrate
your shattered mind

Slowly bitterness and anger
Seeps into your troubled mind
In your soul you wonder
Why were you the one left behind

RIK

People who are stuck on themselves
never get the point.

Don't only have pride on how you look
have pride on how you live.

So often we learn too late
the important things in life.
"Would'a, Could'a, Should'a."

Treat every day as a given, that's what
makes our tomorrows worth liven.

Longevity is worth more than gold.

Don't just glance at the words
written on the wall, stare at their meaning.

Gospel Music
Makes you holler
Makes you shout
Helps you let
Your feelings out

Blues
It makes you sad
It lets you down
It slowly turns
Your soul around

Rock & Roll
It's loud and it's snappy
Makes your whole body happy

Jazz
The sound is smooth, fast, cool,
sometimes slow
It meditates
It soothes the soul

Country
It tells stories, sad, happy and true
It really takes hold of you
You can feel it from head to feet
As those country boots stomp
to the beat

Reggae
Notes are happy they have a charm
Makes you smile makes you warm
Lets yourself know just how you feel
Those rhythmic sounds from
drums of steel

Sadness for those who hear the music
but don't feel it.

My dog keeps telling me
"It's a RUFF life."

SENILE
"I don't understand Uncle Willy anymore.

Every time I visit him, he's either alone
or with somebody.

Computers are contagious.

Ladies know how much perfume,
Men will make you short of breath.

You can plant a tree, however,
only the Lord can make it grow
(Margret Beatrice Turner/Aunt)

Shake my hand, don't squeeze it.

A smile is contagious.

Instead of being color struck,
be color blind.

Diversity paints a wonderful rainbow.

Turn your thoughts to heaven
and your deeds to earth.

Don't give it to me,
let me earn it.

Life is a gift, be thankful,
do something with it.

You put your foot in this meal,
guess that's why it stinks so good.

Why are all rabbits named Jack?

Having a crush on someone
doesn't mean you want to flatten them.

Water seeks its own level and
a wet bird never flies at night!

Elephants never forget.
How do we know?

Lottery
You can't play the number,
the number has to play you!

UKRAIN: And the world stood by!

At night; why do people turn
the TV on to go to sleep, wake up in the morning
and turn it off? They haven't watched a damn thing;
ALL NIGHT?

"Strike Three"
1st Umpire: Some are balls, some are strikes
I call them as I see them.
2'nd Umpire: Some are balls, some are strikes
I call them, as they are.

3'rd Umpire: Some are balls, some are strikes
they ain't nothing until I them.

You need to get your shit together.
I'm not putting my hands on any stinky
ass shit to get it together.

You can't remember what you forgot.
You can't force your memory
but you can retain your thoughtfulness.

Have you ever been so drunk you couldn't
grab the bed when it came around the first time?

If you ever whished upon a star,
your ass would be cinders right now.

Has a stork ever dropped a baby en route?

Is your spouse having an affair
with Bengay? What's it mean when you replace
Chanel #5 and Old Spice with Bengay?

After age 65, a one nighter is
the number of times you
took a trip to the bathroom.

Don't just look at it, do something about it.

It's a sin to be lazy, it should be a crime.

Words to live bye certainly don't come from me!
I'm writing fast because life is short.

People who sleep their life away
are breathing but not living.

"Under every stone, lurks a politician."
(Aristophanes)

Count from one hundred backwards.
Why?

Every book has an ending, this one is getting close!

Some problems are big, some problems are small.
Being one person you can solve some but,
you can't solve them all.

Carpentry
I was cutting a new door for my shed.
My next door neighbors, John and Jo Miller
shouted, "Rick, measure twice before you
cut once." "Ooops."
I didn't listen.

My wife, using profanity in a shallow tone; Gwen, what
did you just say. Rick I was scolding the dog.
The dog was outside.

I ask my partner. "George, what's it like to bungee jump?"
"Rick, damned if I know, my eyes were closed the
whole darn time."
(George Edmonds/Police partner)

You can build it but it's never
finished until you paint it.

Prayer is the power of belief.
Crossing fingers is the power of hope.
Leave it to the Almighty to do his work.

GOLDEN YEARS

Remember how we looked forward
to the golden years
All that they have brought us
is funerals, aches, pain and tears

Now as we look forward to tomorrow
We wonder what it will bring us
happiness or sorrow

Not to many old friends
we can call on the phone
More than too many
have left us all alone

It's a great challenge to go
to church or the grocery store get
driver phobia
Don't have the skills
to drive safely anymore

Don't understand all this
thing called "High Tech"
I'm computer illiterate
Grandkids tried to teach me
but I'm too old to get it

How I loved the young years
They were so much fun
in these GOLDEN YEARS
all of that is done

Perfume use to be Chanel #5
had to switch to Bengay
it helps me stay alive
Well I have to close now
got a doctor's appointment
Gonna hitch a ride
get a prescription and some
rubbing ointment Rik

A LITTLE MIXED UP

Just a line to say I'm living,
that I'm not among the dead.
Though I'm getting more forgetful
and more mixed up in the head.

For sometimes I can't remember
when I stand at the foot of the stairs.
Was I going up for something
or have I just come down from there?

And before the frig so often
my poor mind is filled with doubt.
Have I just put food away
or have I come to take some out.

Then there are times when it's dark out
and with my nightcap on my head,
I don't know if I'm retiring
or just getting out of bed.

So, if it's my turn to write you,
there's no need for getting sore.
I may think that I have written
and don't want to be a bore.

So remember: I do love you
and I wish that you were here.
But now it's nearly mail time
so I must say "Good-by dear"

Here I stand beside the mailbox
with my face so very red.
Instead of mailing you the letter
I've opened it instead.
(unknown)

"Never look a gift horse in the mouth."
Can someone explain this to me?
Reindeer are the only animals that
bring gifts!

A lesson taught is a lesson learned.

Do you stir it up or do you stir it around?
(You can stir up trouble)

To all backseat drivers.
Where do you sit in a two-seater?

Your mind is what you control.
Your brain controls its self.

To all of us drinkers a Dirty Martini means
the glass isn't clean.

A fatal mistake, not believing
things are as bad as they really are.

My favorite restaurants
are "Doggie Baggies"
(Bow Wow Me Up)

"Don't cry over spilled milk."
Cry over lost money.

Do Comedians ever cry?

Nutrition
I love my vegetables, love them, but I'll never,
eat those "Jolly Green Giant" vegetables!
Why?
Because he stands over all that corn and PEAS!
(Melvin "Slappy" White/ Friend/Comedian)

RETIREMENT
Wake up in the morning, read the obituary
and if I'm not dead. I fix my cup of coffee
and get my ass back into bed.

OLD AGE
Taking a walk means going to the bathroom.

Are you one of those readers that
will catch on next week?

Some people acquire beautiful real estate
and turn it into a "Section Eight."

There are times in life that we make
a wrong turn, avoid making too many.

FISHERMAN'S PRAYER
God grant that I may live to fish
For another shining day
But when my final cast is made
I then most humbly pray.

When nestled in your landing net
As I lay peacefully asleep
You'll smile at me and judge
That I'm "good enough to keep."

(KIP Price/Friend)

'THE GOOD OLD DAYS'

I didn't forget, I just remembered

Were they really so Good? Let's Reminisce

Woolworths and Newberry was the shopping mall. The dentist was a string and doorknob tied to your tooth. The "Tooth Fairy" didn't show up. The clothes dryer was a rope with sticks. The bathtub was a tin bucket; the only two soaps were Lifebuoy and Ivory. An ice cube was a chip off the block. Ice cream only had three flavors. Snow cones didn't have a spoon. A soda pop was seven cents, you only had a nickel, the barber's clippers hurt your scalp and hot combs were torture. When it snowed tires wore chains that broke. Remember the "Potty." Movies had no color. Washboards had ridges. "Jim Crow" was America's Hero. I'm just getting started.

Boy's pants only came to their knees to meet their long socks. Corsets and girdles were a pain in the butt. Stockings had tight garters that cut off circulation. Homemade slingshots were BB guns. The ice cream truck was the event of the day. Castor oil cured every ailment and mercurochrome healed a cut throat. Shoe strings broke, there was always a hole in the sole, you repaired shoes rather than buying new ones. You rolled your cigarettes by hand and spit. Mumblety-pegs, checkers, cards, hop scotch, hide-go-seek and jacks were the only games. A Drive-By was not stopping at Fritsch's for a Big Boy. Conk set your head ablaze. Skates had straps that cut your legs. Cars had cozy wings for air, hand rolled windows, a clutch and you drove with both hands and two feet. Baseball bats were sawed off broom sticks. You shoveled coal to stay warm. Lawn mowers were powered by hand. Down south lynch mobs was a sporting event. "Hold on," I'm not finished.

Street cars gave you a headache. You had to read and write to buy liquor. You're only writing tools were a pen, pencil and an ink well. No back packs for schoolbooks. You told time by the growl in your stomach or the house call, a long drawn out "Sonny," meant get your ass home. Gas was twenty five cents a gallon but you didn't have a car yet. Remember oil lamps and pot belly stoves. Every teacher had a paddle, every yard had a switch. Grass had chiggers and almost every kid had mumps, measles, chickenpox or ringworm. They pulled your tonsils for no good reason. The only shower was a fire hydrant or a garden hose. A blender was an egg beater. The only birth control was a "rain coat." Minimum wage was less than $1.00 an hour. Maybe, just maybe, those "GOOD OLD DAYS" weren't so GOOD after All.

Dr. Richard "Rick" Rhodes "2020"

Take one step at a time.
Ok, what time?

I'm calling Angie's List to see who can put me back together.

There are good times, bad times and
hard times but no soft times.

It's easier to be nice than nasty.

You can't control alcohol.
Alcohol controls you.

"Hold that question."
"Ok, hold that answer,
asshole.
(In your hand)

Basketball is the only basket that
has a hole with a purpose.

I can only write or paint when
I'm in the mood. My life is a mood.

Absent Minded
Your brain is missing at roll call.

Millions and millions of prayers
go unanswered every day.

The uneducated ask what.
The educated ask why.
The non-educated just wonders.

It's not how much you save.
It's important you learn to save.

Dis & Dat
Sometime we get "dis" confused with "dat".
Just remember, "dis" is more important than "dat."

Sometimes we don't see ourselves,
it takes others to tell us what we look like.

If a free society cannot help the many that are
poor, it cannot save the few that are rich.
(John F. Kennedy)

Let us never negotiate out of fear.
But let us never fear to negotiate.
(John F. Kennedy)

If a man hasn't discovered something he
will die for, he isn't fit to live.
(Rev. Martin Luther King)

You may fool all of the people some of the time;
you can even fool some of the people all of the time;
but you can't fool all of the people all of the time.
(Abraham Lincoln)

Injustice anywhere is a threat to justice everywhere.
(Dr. Martin Luther King)

Host
"Can I fix you a drink?"
"I don't drink any more, however,
I don't drink any less either."

Word Games
YET: a funny useless word.
Have you washed the car yet?
Have you been to the doctor yet?
I have yet to do either.
Yet is a busy person.
Why not!
Have you washed the car?
Have you been to the doctor?
Why not just say no, rather than;
no not yet. Let's give yet a last name.

I only drink on days that end with Y.

"Fuck, excuse my French!"
Why blame the French on your foul mouth?
Why not the Germans, Italians,
Chinese, etc.?

You screwed me up. Up where, did it hurt?
Most things are screwed down, or together.

Is your body qualified for membership
in the "Hoopty" club?

Why take a shower when you
like the way you stink?

Why complain about the mail carrier
being late and only open your mail
every other week.

When all is said and done
may your life become
a long letter rather than a
short note.

Marriage is not a 50/50 partnership, it's
a 100/100 partnership. You give all
I give all.
(Ron Jones/friend)

Dusty's recent doctors visit he was told he was improving. "Just keep doing whatever you've been doing and you'll be ok." So he left the doctor's office, went to the liquor store and purchased a bottle of vodka.

I smelled gas so I struck a match. "Where are you now?"

Some people have a smart brain and a stupid ass. Malfunction below deck.

Don't let your own self get in your way. (Mike Tyson)

Phone Call
(Ring, Ring) "Hey Dusty, what's up?" "Nothing dad, just flying around with the Grey Goose." Well pluck me a few feathers, I'm on my way over.

"Brief orders, speeches that are too long are likely to be forgotten. (Abu Bakr)

Life is short, then you die.

My wife told me I looked extra fine in my Sunday best. I'm now thinking of never changing clothes.

Has the cat got your tongue?
WHAT?

Oh go jump in the lake.
Why?

Ghost Words
Conversations with Walter Darton, my cousin.
Almost everything I say he responds, "Rick you
outa quit." If I quit as many times as he told me;
I'd have no sex, booze, parties, fun or even trouble.
Walt, "You outa quit."
(See addendum)

Very few are born gifted,
No one is born smart!

Nothing bounces like a football or a bad check.

You can never catch up with procrastination.

Have no problem with dying,
after death there are no problems.

Dusty Rhodes married Debbie Lane
and they journeyed both ROADS
together.
(Memories of Debbie)

Remember
SANDY HOOK, etc.

Good Coach/Bad Coach
Keep playing like you've been playing
we'll get into the record book.
Zero wins and twenty loses.

"That sucks."
VULGAR
Mind your manners!

I can only write or paint when
I'm in the mood, my whole life
is a mood.

Eight Precious Words
Count on me
Peace of mind
Love you

Remember
(DEMOCRACY)

"Jim Crow"
I have personally been a victim of
segregated bathrooms and drinking fountains.
Georgia's back of the bus and train rule.
Eaten in a cubby hole served
through a hole in the wall.
Denied the choice of a drinking fountain.
(Water is water)

A victim of Jim Crow in four states,
West Virginia, Ohio, Kentucky and
Georgia. Jim Crow breeds anger.
Still, I love my country.

If you never take a chance
you'll never be a winner.

If you can't spell, you can't read.

Why can't I have my cake and eat it too?
If you have your cake you can do with it
whatever you want.

(My cousins)
Walter: "Maesoa why can't I get a dog?"
Maesoa: "Because one dog in this house
is one too many."

What was it like being a soldier and a police officer?
The ultimate experiences of my lifetime.

"Is there any one thing you'd
like to do over and over again?"

HAVE SEX
Some people have multiple choices in life
be grateful, some have none.

Jealousy is a cancer that kills within.
To be a "Do Nothing"
means you don't exist.

A new page in life doesn't always
have to be a happy one.

Why do some people swear on
their mother's grave when she's still alive
and doesn't have a grave.

Why do we look down to pray
rather than up to heaven?

Why do some people spend more
time sleeping on the sofa than
than in the bed?

Why do some people sleep
with the lights on?

Why is a Colored drinking fountain White?
Water has no color?
(Jim!)

"All gave some
Some gave all."

If you live in a trailer why are you trash?

The pain of the loser is greater
than the joy of the winner.

Fashion is not what you want to wear.
It's what someone told you to wear.

On occasion reward yourself
feel good about who you are.
Some coaches coach the game.
Some coaches know the game.
(Amen)

Did you ever think how great it
might be to live a dog's life?
(Think about it)
"RUFF"

What's the difference between a
couch potato and a couch tomato or couch apple?
(vegetable/fruit)
They're all do nothings!

Why do we have proper English?
No one uses it!

The best way to find you is to lose yourself

"Yesterday is History
Today's a Blessing
Tomorrow's a Mystery."
(Mike Ditka) Chicago Bear's coach
Player

"I've learned that people will forget what you
said, people will forget what you did, but
people will never forget how you made them feel."
(Maya Angelo)

"Darkness cannot drive out the darkness; only
light can do that. Hate cannot drive out hate;
only love can do that."
(Martin Luther King Jr.)

"If I can help someone as I pass this way
Then my living shall not be in vain."
(Martin Luther King Jr.)

Phone Chat
Rick: Walt, I start watching the sport games, however,
I fall asleep before the end, I never knew who won.
Walt: Rick, damn who won, at our age just
worry about "WAKING UP."

This book was not intended
to offend anyone, if it did, FUCK'EM.

THAT'S ALL FOLKS

*To my wife "Gwen," I'll never stop
Writing, Painting or
Loving You.*

TWO SHORT STORIES

New Year Tradition
The new year is quickly approaching, I'm turning
this manuscript in the first of the year. There's a
traditional Black's folk new year menu derived from slavery,
mainly scraps. In Paris France, there lies a world
famous restaurant, Gabby (French lady) Haynes (Black GI).
They met during WWII and started the restaurant.
I ate a least one meal there every day while in Paris.
It's small, subdued non décor, strictly, mom & pop.
Celebrity customers pictures cover the walls
Frank Sinatra, Louis Armstrong, Tony Bennett, Elvis,
Jackie Gleason and others.

(MENU jargon)
Pig Feet...................Trotters
Pan Cakes...............Blow Out Patches
Bacon.....................Tire Tracks
Chitterlings.............City Wrinkles
Black-eyed Peas.....Hoppin' Johns
(on & on)

New year eve Gwen ask me to grocery
shop for pig tails which we love to BBQ,
not being particular about the feet.
I returned without them. "Where's the pig tails,"
she ask, "Sold out I replied."
"Well did you get some feet?"
"No, I'd rather have some tail than
some feet any day."

Don't eat that pork!
"Damn that, I love my pork so much
I even eat the OINK."
(Redd Foxx)

New year menu for many Southern folk.
Pig feet, yams, collard greens, black-eyed peas/
hoppin' john, mac & cheese, corn bread and grease.
"Yum Yum"

"Hoppin' John"
A traditional southern dish eaten on New Year day
And luck will follow you the rest of the year. It dates back to
the 1800s. The name changes to Skippin' Jenny the following days
when leftovers are eaten days after. Black-eyed peas represents
coins. Collard green, greenbacks, cornbread gold, pork, ham
hocks and chitterlings, the cheap meats provided to enslaved people.

It is believed the recipe was created by people from Africa who
were enslaved on the Sea Islands off the coast of Carolina and
Georgia. It is considered a cuisine in North and South Carolina.
One source suggest that "Hoppin' John" was a handicapped man
who cooked and sold the dish in Charleston, South Carolina, A
More Dubois explanation suggest that in South Carolina it
was customary to invite a guest to dinner by saying "Hop in John."

The reason this is in the book, it's December, close to
January and fitting. The book goes to the publisher next week.

A Happening

The year, 1961, neither of us knew each other at the time. Michael "Hap" O'Daniel, a young aspiring Xavier college student in Cincinnati Ohio. Myself, Rick Rhodes, a rookie cop on Cincinnati Police Department just cut loose from my training officer to patrol solo. Redd Foxx "John Elroy Sanford" a "Blue Joke" Comedian traveling from coast to coast in an old Caddy to perform wherever the venue called.

It was late night or early morning, still dark. An old ten year (1951) green Oldsmobile (hoopty) ran a stop sign. Bang, I got one, what we refer to as a mover, car in motion. Contrary to belief, there is no quota for traffic enforcement on the Cincinnati Police Department. I turned on my flashing lights and began pursuit. After a short pursuit I pulled the car over, the driver was Michael O'Daniel. His story was that he was trying to get home to Louisville Kentucky for the family Thanksgiving affair that morning.

I wrote him a citation and a court date. Naturally he was pissed. I appeared in court on the designated date. Mr. O'Daniel was a "No Show. Being a rookie I wanted to impress my superiors with my activity report. Hindsight, if I would have been a seasoned veteran I would not have tagged him. I felt bad, it bothered me. He called the court in Cincinnati from Louisville and informed them he could not make his court date, car trouble. I believed that. He was granted a continuance. Next court date he informed the judge of his (Hoopty) hardship. I felt bad again, I requested a dismissal, and the judge granted it. Was the incident forgotten? No, it still bothered me, again he was such a nice guy.

Other than my law enforcement occupation I was managing a local girl's trio, "The Jewels." My road manager, Candy Carroll a former drummer for BB King and other noted groups. He was a friend of Redd. Candy was taking the trio on the road, he introduced me to Redd; ask if I would companion him for a few days in his absence. Redd and I hit it off big time. During this time I was an undercover vice squad detective. Redd was impressed with my martial art skills. The two of us socialized visiting soul food restaurants, clubs, and home cooking at the house every time he was in town. He became my youngest son Che's Godfather.

Meanwhile Hap graduated college and procured employment with the Cincinnati Post newspaper as an entertainment journalist. Hap as he is affectionately referred to, covered Redd's engagement. It was at the Living Room, a very nice supper club in downtown Cincinnati. Redd for the most part was getting negative criticism because of his so called "Blue Jokes." Hap wrote a very positive review about Redd's act, something other critics lacked the courage to do. Redd was very appreciative and extremely grateful about the article, he never forgot about it.

Some years later, 1974 after Redd parted ways with his longtime manager, Bardo Ali; Redd contacted Hap and he became Redd's manager. At this point Redd was playing some very upscale dates on the east coast New York, Jersey, and Philly. He ask me to bodyguard him, I responded. After Redd's performance the crew gathered in Redd's hospitality suite. This tall handsome dark haired white guy stood out. He kept staring at me across the room, a somewhat puzzled look on his face. I thought, is this guy gay, or does he think I am? Finally, he crossed the room and sat on the sofa next to me. Not even looking at me he said. "Can't be too many Rick Rhodes on the Cincinnati Police Department can there? Surprised by the comment, I responded, "Got that right." "You gave me a ticket years ago Thanksgiving morning on Kemper Lane approaching Columbia Parkway, "one of the most dangerous parkways in the country at the time. With a jerk of my head, I looked at him and said. "Sure did, oh man, that was you!" "Sure was." We laughed, became friendly almost instantly.

Sometime before I had written a small article, "Three Faces of a Genius" about Redd, it was published in a small local newsletter. Someone gave it to Redd, he gave me a positive jester and handed it to Hap. It must have left a tiny impression on Hap, some days later he ask me to write a treatment for a TV sitcom. Somehow, somewhere it got lost in file 13. Hap still believed I could write, I believe he is mistaken. As time passed he kept helping and encouraging me, my mentor. Because of my wife Gwen, Hap and Redd I have just finished this book, my fourth and last. What a coincident.

THANKS to a Special Trio.
Rick,

Eventually I substituted for Hap as Redd's manager, while Hap was attending to business contracts for "Sanford and Son" upcoming season. To this day I know Hap had something to do with my becoming Redd's manager in his absence.

EXCERPTS

From My Book
"I DON'T UNDERSTAND"
(Referred to as the WHY-Book)

How many times a day do you use the word "WHY?"
It is not my intention to be hypercritical. This is not a
questionnaire, instead it is to stimulate the mind of the
reader regarding general and personal WHY questions.

Why is it OK to use the word "Nigger" if you're
Black, but not if you're White?
It's not OK to use it no matter who you are.

Why do we say talk is cheap? I didn't know talk had a price.

Why do squirrels bury their nuts and then can't find them?
Refers to male squirrels only!

Why do we say I have to get my shit together? I'm not
putting my hands on my shit to get it together.

I'm trying to find someone that knows "What" or
"Whys" last name. We're always asking, do you know
What or Why?

Why when having sex we say. "I just came." Came from
where?

Why if you feel horny just get in the car
and blow the horn.

Why life is a bitch and then you have puppies?

Why does going to church make you a Christian?
Why going to the garage doesn't make you a mechanic.

Why beauty salons get more news than TV stations.

Why the sock fairy won't stay out of the washer or dryer?

Why do men lose their Head over a piece of Tail?

Why do we say we are ONE nation under GOD?
There are many nations under GOD.

Why a computer is more intelligent than me and
it never went to school?

Soul food always taste better the next day.
Why is there a "T" after the letter "X"?

Why say I'm gone when I'm still here?

Why is a rabbit's foot good luck if the rabbit lost it?
(Redd Foxx/Friend)

Why we bake an upside down cake and eat it
right side up?

Why is bigger better? I'd rather have a small debt rather
than a big debt. A small problem than a big one.

Why some people have brains that don't work?

Why do track meets, horse and car races
only make left turns?
Why is there a fine line but never a thick line?

Why do we fall asleep, fall off what?
Just go to sleep. Don't hurt yourself!

Why we say, "Hold that thought," have you
ever held a thought in your hand?

Why is there a black sheep in the family
but never a white sheep?

Why we say, "I just lost my mind?"
Look around and find it.

Why I can't write anymore, I'm out of vodka.

Why have rollovers on your vehicle
and don't fasten your seatbelt?

Why do we overburden GOD with selfish
prayers? HE doesn't get overtime pay.

Why are so many people getting VAXED tomorrow?
"Too Late!"

Don't fall asleep, you may hurt yourself.
Just go to sleep.

ADDENDUM

Justice vs. Injustice

These words depict the justices in contrast to the injustices that at some time in our lives; some of us, many of us or maybe, just maybe all of us; no matter, the race color, gender, creed or tribe have experienced.

No matter how big or how small, they are remembered. They cannot be erased, however with courage, determination and dedication; they can become equal, fair and honest.

GOD bless,
Dr. Richard Stewart Rhodes

Age of Enlightenment
17th/18th century

A period that focused on "crime and punishment." One form
of punishment was to put the perpetrator pillory. A wooden
frame in which the head and hands could be locked. Whatever
the crime they were charged with was written above their head,
i.e. Theft, Beggar, etc. The townspeople would throw objects at
them. For a sex crime, "For Unlawful Carnal Knowledge."
The words were too long so they abbreviated them using
the first letter of each word. Later in time predicting
future wars it was persuaded by the king's rule to fornicate,
using the same language. The purpose was to produce
more male births to fight in the oncoming wars.
The same language
for a different reason.

THE BROWNSVILLE AFFAIR
(or Raid)

The incident (1906) was an act of racial discrimination due to resentment by White residents of Brownsville Texas of the Buffalo Soldiers; an African-American unit stationed nearby. (The 25th Infantry Regiment}During the raid a white barber was killed and a White police officer was wounded by gunshots. The towns' people accused the Black soldiers of the raid. Although their commanders said the soldiers were in their barracks all night, evidence was allegedly planted against the soldiers.

As a result of a United States Army Inspector General's investigation President Theodore Roosevelt ordered discharge without honor of 167 solders of the regiment, costing them their pensions and preventing them from ever serving in any federal civil service jobs. The case aroused outrage in both Black and White communities. After further investigation several of the men were allowed to re-enlist.

In early 1970 a renewed military investigation exonerated the discharged Black troops. The government pardoned them in 1972 and restored their honorable records. All of the soldiers received Honorable Discharges, POSTHUMOUSLY!

It Bites My Soul

https://en.wikpedia.org/wiki/brownsville_affair#Evidence

THE BROTHERHOOD CREED

With difficulty I will attempt to describe the presentation of this awesome poem. After all the jokes, laughter and joy, Slappy presents an oral delivery to the audience about Love, Hate and Peace. Putting a White glove on one hand and a Black glove on the other. The stage lights are darkened to pitch black with the exception of each glove which is illuminated. (glowing) The orchestra is playing in a low monotone pitch. In sync with Slappy's voice the gloves move with distinct gestures. In the pin drop silence of the room, the entire audience is mesmerized as he recites the poem. (Unbelievable) A full house standing ovation at every venue. Hopefully you will reread the poem imagining this scenario.

Thanks,
Dr. Rick

Ghost Words

These are a word or words we say during conversation that we don't realize we are saying. They are actually a habit, making no sense to the subject matter. i.e.

"Got cha." "You know." "Right."

"Heard that." "By the way," etc.

What is your ghost word?

"LAND'S END"
Our Home on the Lake

09/04/2005

A place that bites the soul, where normality
is lost, and serenity overcomes all

Where freshness wipes out the mold, the
beauty of winter, spring, summer and fall

Where memories are never lost, they come to life again

The cloudy rainy days fade out, the
golden sun light comes shinning in

Where the tiny whitecaps, on the
clear blue waters prevail

Where a vast assortment of boats,
cast off and set their sail

Where attitudes are lost and friendships begin

This is the place that we have named "LAND'S END"

Now let us close, by saying "AMEN"

Rick Rhodes, 2004

POEMS

SIMONE "Anika" WILSON

The Cake I Ate

A Crack Head's Prayer

Faith

Panhandler

THE CAKE I ATE

Hello scale, my old friend
Here I am, back again.
Don't really want to look at you
For all the hell you put me through
Been on a diet for oh so long
What in the world am I doing wrong?
I eat what I'm supposed to eat
But I still can't see my feet.

Broccoli, lettuce, carrots, kale
I just don't want to face you scale.
Protein smoothies, lemonade
How much progress have I made?
Suck it up and just get on
What! Those numbers must be wrong.

I followed my diet
I stuck to the plan.
I ate only chicken
Left the gravy in the pan.
So what in the world is wrong with my weight?
Oh, now I remember,
It's the cake I ate.

Simone "Anika" Wilson

A CRACKHEAD'S PRAYER

There's a rock in my sock
I got cocaine in my brain
I'm so high right now,
I don't know my name
Five years ago I wanted to fly
Down so low, thought I'd
Give crack a try
Hit that pipe once and I started to soar
I did believe I'd be hooked that day forward
It seemed so tiny and harmless to me
Now I'm in chains; I'm in slavery
The birds don stopped singing
The sky done turned black
I hit the rock once now there's no turning back
Sweat pouring from my brow, begs me ask, "How?"
How do I escape this padded cell
How do I unlock these gates of hell?
I'm running and running I'm trying to flee
Am I chasing it or is it chasing me
I want to soar like I did that first time
But there's no sense of reason, no sense of rhyme
I see people around me but I'm all alone
Dear God I'm tired
I just want to go home

Simone Anika Wilson

FAITH

Faith the substance of things hoped for,
It's the evidence of things not seen.
It means standing strong on God's promise
and never letting go of your dreams.
With your faith you can move mountains
As you're clearing the pathway you trod.
Stretch forward your hands to Jesus.
Like Moses stretched forth his rod.

Each day that God gives you press forward
For your faith will be put to the test.
God said in His world he will reward you.
There's a prize if you put forth your best.
There'll be times when it seems you'll be tempted
And God is nowhere to be found.
Hold tight to your faith unrelenting.
His blessings to you will abound.

Walk hand in hand with the Master
He will supply every need.
The faith that's required is little,
The size of just one mustard seed.
Your light will shine bright in the darkness
The King of Kings shall prevail.
Your faith will declare to all mankind
My God can do anything but fail.

Simone "Anika" Wilson

PANHANDLER

What you got your hand out for?
Hanging out in front the store
Stopping folks as they pass by,
How bout working?
Give that a try.

I work ten hours every day.
Me and my kids have to make our way.
Here's a newsflash you see,
I don't give men money,
They give it to me.

Simone Anika Wilson

IN MEMORY
Raymond Kinney Cooper
Mr. R.K.
A very special elder, a few words from his books.

TAKE NOT THE EASY WAY
Privileges should be earned
Life owes no man a living

In English man is taught
the harshest words are
I'VE BEEN CAUGHT
Dec/10/1973

He who wears his feelings on his
coat sleeves will soon need a
new jacket
Dec/3/1974

ANSWERS
Although I say I won't get old
It takes hard work with spirit bold
An interest surrounding life
Be it peace or be it strife.
The physical often hits a wall
Too strong to push – to climb too tall,
Rest your body – stir your mind
Many answers you will find.
Feb/27/1976

MUSIC
Laughter is the world's sweetest music
And good humor is the orchestra
Sept/1969

TOMORROW

Tomorrow is a funny day
It never quite gets here
And still we have plan for it
Because it is so near

Its' hours from us is twenty-four
And sometimes many less
They say it meets today at night
While I'm asleep I guess

Some people say it won't arrive
They waste their time and play
Perhaps they'd like Tomorrow best
If they would work today.
March/15/1968

FEAR

I fear me things I cannot do
The things I would or should
Perhaps but I should drop my fear
These things and more I could.

Most times it's Future that I fear
The things that may go wrong
When something seems to needle me
They say "you're weak not strong"

My patience must be more than those
Who have to win right now
I'll try it once ten-times and more
Until its right I vow.

But though I fear I will be brave
I'll charge the enemy
No matter where or what or who
It's conqueror I'll be.
Oct/1969

Sir, may you always be among the clouds.
Rickey

Mr. Leroy Carroll

Writings

Born Before 1945

Getting Older

Born Before Even After
(1945)

Believe it or not, many of us were born before or soon after 1945.
If you happen to be a proud member of this group,
consider the changes we have witnessed. If not a member,
read it anyway, you may find it interesting!
Check this out.
We were born before television, before penicillin, before polio shots,
frozen food, Xerox, plastic, contact lenses, Frisbees and the pill.

We were born before radar, credit cards, split atoms, lazier
beams, ballpoint pens, before panty hose, dishwashers,
clothes dryers, electric blankets, air conditioners, drip-
dry clothes and before man walked on the moon.
We got married first and then lived together.

Bunnies were small rabbits and rabbits were not Volkswagens. Designer
jeans scheming girls named Jean and Jeannie. Having a meaningful
relationship meant getting along with our cousins.

We thought fast food was what you ate during lent.

We were born before house-husbands; gay rights, computer dating, dual
careers and computer marriages. We were born before day-care centers,
group therapy and nursing homes, We never heard of FM radio, tape decks,
electric typewriters, artificial hearts, food and word processors, yogurt
and guys wearing earrings. For us "Time Sharing" meant togetherness.
Hard ware meant a store and software wasn't even a word! When a
#10 tub meant you were about to take a bath or your cloths were being
washed. A chip meant a piece of wood, When the toilet seat sprung up at
the same time the toilet flushed, sometimes you had to pull the overhead
chain to flush it.; some toilets were on the outside. "Brrruuuuuuu"

HOW DO YOU KNOW YOU'RE GETTING OLDER?

Everything hurts and what doesn't hurt doesn't work
The gleam in your eye is the sun hitting your bifocals
You feel like the night before and you haven't been anywhere
Your little black book contains only names ending in MD
You get winded playing cards
You join the health club and don't go
You know all the answers, but no one ask you any questions
You need glasses to find your glasses
You turn out the lights for economic rather than romantic reasons
You sit in the rocking chair and can't get it going
Your knees buckle but your belt won't
Your back goes out more than you do
You have too much room in the house and not enough in the medicine cabinet
You sink your teeth in to a steak a000000nd they stay there
You visit the doctor's office childhood friends from your old neighborhood
"YOU WONDER WHY MORE PEOPLE DON'T USE THIS SIZE PRINT"

(Leroy Carroll/ Friend)

"Kritic's Korner"

It runs the gauntlet of life! Uniquely written, educational, bites the funny bone, a real page turner. Don't just look at the cover, read the book.

About The Author

Dr. Richard Stewart "Rick" Rhodes is an army veteran,
served on the Cincinnati Police Department 30 years,
Police Sergeant, (Ret). Assistant Police Chief, Taft Oklahoma,
Professor University of Cincinnati, 20 years, (Ret)
Co-founder of Sentinels, a Black police officer's organization.
As a police officer he survived two face to face gun fights: for
which he received the city's highest award for bravery and valor.

Founder and CEO of his security company,
Amalgamated Security Services, Inc. President,
Coalition of Neighborhoods, Cincinnati, Ohio.
Bodyguard / manager to the late Redd Foxx,
bodyguard to Rev. Jesse Jackson. Commander State of Ohio:
Concern Veterans from Vietnam. Previous books:
"I Don't Understand." His own biography: "Gun Badge and Cuffs."
"Blanket" (Adventures of a boy and his dog).
He loves adventures and challenges; sky diving, professional
scuba diving. Karate (national competition) and international travel.
Commitment to managing his wife Gwen, a jazz singer.

He is a 32nd degree Mason and Shriner Sinai Temple #59
Hobbies include, painting, writing, fishing; a thirst for knowledge.
An adornment to nature and most recently learning the art of Tai Chi.
His Love: Wife, family, friends and life at his lake home. (Memories)

"Peace of Mind"

Paintings

Jamaica Sunset

Land's End

Midnight Sea

My Favorite Cove

Northern Stream

On the Rocks

Printed in the United States
by Baker & Taylor Publisher Services